Machine Learning with Python

Fundamentals

Epris E. Ezekiel

Copyright 2024© Epris E. Ezekiel

All rights reserved. This book is copyrighted and no part of it may be reproduced, distributed, or transmitted in any form or by any means, including photocopying, recording, or other electronic or mechanical methods, without the prior written permission of the publisher, except in the case of brief quotations embodied in critical reviews and certain other non-commercial uses permitted by copyright law.

**Printed in the United States of America
Copyright 2024© Epris E. Ezekiel**

Contents

Introduction 1

Chapter 1 2

What is machine learning? 2

Chapter 2 6

Types of Machine Learning... 6

Chapter 3 13

Understanding the impact of machine learning. 13

Chapter 4 17

Why Python Machine Learning? 17

Chapter 5 25

What Are the Most Challenging Parts of Learning Python for Machine Learning? 25

Chapter6 28

Mastering Python for Machine Learning 28

Final Thoughts... 32

Introduction

Understanding the tools that fuel innovation is no longer a luxury, but rather a requirement in this age of digital transformation. Machine learning is one of the technologies driving this revolution. This article seeks to demystify machine learning by offering a detailed guide for both beginners and aficionados. We will look at the definition of machine learning, its various types, applications, and technologies utilized in the field. We will also discuss the many career pathways in machine learning and offer advice on how to get started in this exciting industry.

If you're considering starting your adventure into Machine Learning, you've heard about Python's adaptability, which can help you comprehend Machine Learning more effectively. Python has become the world's fastest-growing language due to its widespread use in industries and the ability to combine Python with other languages to provide faster and more accurate results.

Chapter 1

What is machine learning?

Machine Learning (ML) is a subset of artificial intelligence (AI) that focuses on the creation of computer algorithms that improve automatically via experience and the usage of data. Simply said, machine learning allows computers to learn from data and make judgments or predictions without being specifically programmed to do so.

Machine learning is fundamentally about developing and implementing algorithms that facilitate these decisions and predictions. These algorithms are designed to improve with time, becoming more precise and effective as they handle more data. Traditional programming involves a machine following a set of established instructions to complete a task. However, with machine learning, the computer is given a series of examples (data) and a task to complete, but it is up to the computer to determine how to do the task based on the examples provided.

For example, if we want a computer to recognize photographs of cats, we don't give it detailed instructions on what a cat looks like. Instead, we feed it hundreds of photos of cats and allow the machine learning algorithm to identify the common patterns and traits that distinguish a cat. Over time, as the system examines more photographs, it improves its ability to recognize cats, even when given previously unknown images.

Machine learning is extremely powerful and versatile because it can learn from data and improve over time. It is the driving force behind many of today's technological developments, including voice assistants, recommendation systems, self-driving cars, and predictive analytics.

Importance of Machine Learning.

In the twenty-first century, data is the new oil, and machine learning powers this data-driven world. It is an essential technology in today's digital age, and its significance cannot be underestimated. This is reflected in the industry's predicted expansion, with the US Bureau of Labor Statistics forecasting a 21% increase in employment between 2021 and 2031.

Here's why it's so important in the modern world:

- ❖ **Enabling automation:** Machine learning is a critical enabler of automation. Machine learning algorithms, which learn from data and improve over time, can undertake formerly manual activities, enabling humans to focus on more difficult and creative work. This not only improves productivity but also creates new opportunities for creativity.

- ❖ **Driving innovation:** Machine learning is driving innovation and efficiency in a variety of fields. Here are some instances:

  - ✓ The approaches used have applications in fields as diverse as agriculture, education, and entertainment.

  - ✓ Retail. Machine learning has the potential to improve recommendation systems, supply networks, and customer service.

  - ✓ Healthcare. Algorithms are used to forecast disease outbreaks, tailor patient treatment programs, and enhance medical imaging accuracy.

- ✓ Finance. Credit scoring, algorithmic trading, and fraud detection are all examples of machine learning applications.

- ❖ **Data processing:** One of the key reasons machine learning is significant is its capacity to handle and interpret massive amounts of data. Traditional data analysis approaches have proven insufficient as digital data from social media, sensors, and other sources has grown in quantity. Machine learning algorithms can process massive volumes of data, identify hidden patterns, and deliver useful insights to inform decision-making.

Chapter 2

Types of Machine Learning

Machine learning can be divided into three categories based on the nature of the learning system and the data available: supervised learning, unsupervised learning, and reinforcement learning. Let us look into each of these:

Reinforcement Learning
Reinforcement learning is a sort of machine learning in which an agent learns to make decisions through interaction with its surroundings. The agent is awarded or penalized (with points) for its activities, to maximize the total payout.
Reinforcement learning, unlike supervised and unsupervised learning, is best suited to issues where the input is sequential and the decisions made at each stage influence future outcomes. Reinforcement learning is commonly used in gameplay, robotics, resource management, and other applications.

Supervised learning

Supervised learning is the most popular type of machine learning. In this method, the model is trained using a labeled dataset. In other words, the data is accompanied by a label, which the model attempts to predict. This could range from a category name to a real-valued number. During the training process, the model learns a mapping from the input (features) to the output (label). Once trained, the model can anticipate the output of fresh, previously unknown data.

Linear regression, logistic regression, decision trees, and support vector machines are common supervised learning techniques for regression problems and classification problems, respectively. In practice, this could resemble an image recognition process in which a supervised model can correctly recognize and categorize new photographs from a dataset of images labeled as "cat," "dog," and so on.

Unsupervised Learning

In contrast, unsupervised learning includes training the model on an unlabeled dataset. The model is allowed to discover patterns and relationships in the data on its own. This method of learning is frequently used for clustering and dimensionality reduction. Clustering entails grouping related data points, whereas dimensionality reduction entails lowering the number of random variables under consideration by identifying a collection of primary variables.

Common unsupervised learning algorithms include k-means for grouping and Principal Component Analysis (PCA) for dimensionality reduction. Unsupervised learning is commonly used in marketing to segment a company's consumer base. The algorithm can divide clients into segments with comparable behaviors without the use of pre-existing labels by analyzing purchasing habits, demographic data, and other information.

How does machine learning work?
Understanding how machine learning works entails going through a step-by-step process that converts raw data into valuable insights. Let's break down the process:

Step 1: Predictions and deployment.
Once trained and improved, the model is ready to generate predictions based on new data. This procedure entails feeding new data into the model and utilizing the model's output for decision-making or additional analysis. Integrating the model into a production environment allows it to process real-world data and deliver real-time insights. This approach is commonly referred to as MLOps. Learn more about MLOps in a separate tutorial.

Step 2: Evaluate the model.
Once the model has been trained, it is critical to assess its performance before deploying it. This entails testing the model on new data that it did not encounter during training.

Accuracy (for classification problems), precision and recall (for binary classification problems), and mean squared error (for regression problems) are some of the most common metrics used to evaluate model performance.

Step 3: Hyperparameter Tuning and Optimization

After evaluating the model, you may need to change the hyperparameters to increase its performance. This procedure is referred to as parameter tuning or hyperparameter optimization.

Grid search (trying out alternative parameter combinations) and cross-validation (dividing your data into subgroups and training your model on each subset to ensure it performs well on varied data) are two hyperparameter tuning techniques.

Step 4: Data Preprocessing.

Data preparation is an important stage in the machine learning process. It includes cleaning the data (removing duplicates and fixing errors), dealing with missing data (removing or filling it in), and normalizing the data (scaling it to a standard format). Preprocessing enhances the quality of your data and guarantees that your machine-learning model interprets it correctly. This step can considerably increase the accuracy of your model. Our Python course, Preprocessing for Machine Learning, teaches you how to clean your data before modeling it.

Step 5: Selecting the appropriate model.
Once the data has been prepared, the next step is to select a machine-learning model. There are numerous model types to choose from, including linear regression, decision trees, and neural networks. The type of model you use is determined by the nature of your data and the problem you're trying to address. When picking a model, consider the number and kind of your data, the problem's complexity, and the computational resources available. A second post will explain the various machine-learning models in greater detail.

Step 6: Train the model.
After selecting a model, the following step is to train it on the prepared data. Training is the process of feeding data into a model and allowing it to alter its internal parameters to better anticipate the outcome.

During training, it is critical to avoid overfitting (where the model performs well on training data but badly on fresh data) and underfitting.

Step 7: Data Collection

The initial phase in the machine learning process is data collection. Data is the lifeblood of machine learning; the quality and quantity of your data have a direct impact on your model's performance. Data can be acquired from a variety of sources, including databases, text files, pictures, audio recordings, and web scraping. Once acquired, the data must be formatted for machine learning. This procedure entails organizing the data in a proper format, such as a CSV file or a database, as well as ensuring that the data is relevant to the problem being solved.

Chapter 3

Understanding the impact of machine learning.

Machine learning has had a profound impact on many industries, disrupting established procedures and clearing the path for innovation. Let's look at some of these impacts:

Transportation
The revolution in self-driving cars revolves around machine learning. Companies such as Tesla and Waymo utilize machine learning algorithms to evaluate sensor data in real-time, enabling their vehicles to recognize objects, make judgments, and navigate roadways autonomously. Similarly, the Swedish Transport Administration has lately begun collaborating with computer vision and machine learning experts to improve the country's road infrastructure management.

Healthcare
Machine learning is used in healthcare to anticipate disease outbreaks, tailor patient

treatment programs, and increase imaging accuracy. For example, Google's DeepMind Health is collaborating with clinicians to develop machine-learning models that will detect diseases earlier and enhance patient care.

Finance

Machine learning has also improved the financial sector significantly. Its applications include credit scoring, algorithmic trading, and fraud detection. According to a recent poll, 56% of global executives have developed financial crime compliance programs using artificial intelligence (AI) and machine learning.

Some Applications of Machine Learning

Machine learning applications are all around us, often operating in the background to improve our daily lives. Here are some real-world examples:

Voice Assistants

Voice assistants such as Siri, Alexa, and Google Assistant employ machine learning to interpret your voice instructions and respond appropriately. They are always learning from your interactions and improving their performance.

Fraud detection

Banks and credit card issuers employ machine learning to identify fraudulent transactions. They can detect suspicious activities in real-time by assessing typical and abnormal behavior patterns. We offer a fraud detection in Python course that goes over the idea in more detail.

Recommendation systems

Recommendation systems are among the most apparent applications of machine learning. Machine learning is used by companies such as Netflix and Amazon to assess your prior behavior and offer products or movies that you may enjoy. **Python for Machine Learning.**

Python is a popular machine-learning language due to its simplicity and readability, making it ideal for novices. It also features a robust ecosystem of libraries designed for machine learning. Data manipulation and analysis are performed using libraries such as NumPy and Pandas, while data visualization is accomplished using Matplotlib. Scikit-learn offers a diverse set of machine learning techniques, while TensorFlow and PyTorch are used to create and train neural networks.

Python takes three to four times less time to code than other programming languages to get the same outcomes. Python has simpler syntaxes and less complicated functions, emphasizing natural language. Python is frequently the first language newbies learn due to its ease of use.

"Python allows us to produce maintainable features in record times, with a minimum of developers" - Cuong Do, Software Architect for YouTube

According to experts, Python is one of the most important programming languages for machine learning. It is increasingly becoming the preferred solution for any developer working in Big Data, AI, or ML. What distinguishes it as a potential alternative to machine learning?

Chapter 4

Why Python Machine Learning?

Machine Learning Experts frequently work with complex algorithms and clustered data. Python's simplified syntax enables specialists to spend more time solving complicated ML problems rather than focusing on the language's complexity.

Python is an easy language to learn. When exposed to computer science, the majority of secondary school pupils use Python as their primary programming coding language. Anyone with a basic understanding of English and mathematics can start learning Python. Models for machine learning are easier to design because people understand them better.

An extensive array of libraries and frameworks

One of the reasons Python is such a popular choice, in general, is the abundance of libraries and frameworks that make writing easier and save development time. Machine learning and deep learning are particularly well supported.

NumPy, SciPy, and sci-kit-learn are among the most popular libraries, working alongside frameworks such as TensorFlow, CNTK, and Apache Spark. In terms of machine learning and deep learning, these libraries and frameworks are primarily Python-based, with some, such as PyTorch, created particularly for Python.

Better outcomes, i.e. predictions, necessitate the simultaneous compilation of correct data analysis, mathematics, and other features, which Python Machine Learning accomplishes with ease by utilizing publicly available modules.

A library in any programming language is a collection of predefined functions that make it easier to create programs.

Here are some popular libraries for AI and machine learning:

- ✓ For general purpose analysis - Pandas.

- ✓ Machine Learning: Keras, TensorFlow, and Scikit

- ✓ For Data Analysis – NumPy

- ✓ For Advanced Computing – SciPy

- ✓ For data visualization - Seaborn

When working with complex machine learning applications, these libraries assist Machine Learning Engineers in reducing development time and increasing productivity.

After the data has been assembled, it must be displayed concisely; Python Machine Learning covers this task as well, using data visualization attributes.

The simplicity

Python is well-known for its succinct, understandable code, and it is practically unparalleled in terms of use and simplicity, especially for new developers. This has various benefits for machine and deep learning.

Abundant assistance

Python is an open-source programming language with a wealth of tools and excellent documentation. It also has a huge and active developer community that may provide advice and assistance at any level of the development process.

Python is free to use and distribute because it was developed under an OSI-approved open-source license. In this approach, Python allows members of the Python development community to exchange ideas while also encouraging ever-better technological advancements. Thus, the primary benefits of utilizing free Python include education and cost savings.

It is versatile.

Python is a versatile programming language used for a variety of purposes, including web development and data research. How can we explain Python's present rise in these fields? We may look at the increase in traffic from the most popular Python packages. People are developing the collection and code stack of many open-source repositories (which are currently in progress) to continuously improve on existing approaches.

Stack Overflow reports that pandas are by far the fastest-growing Python package. It was introduced only in 2011, but it accounts for 1% of all Stack Overflow question views. As a result, it appears that the advent of data science is a primary driving force behind Python's growth as a programming language.

Simple automation of tasks
Python is popular for automating a variety of tasks. Various packages and scripts enable the automation of any task, including repetitive administrative activities, emailing, and sending HTTP requests. Python can be used to automate blog promotion by promoting articles on Facebook groups or Quora. Chatbots are another helpful automation that can improve customer experience and is possible to implement with Python. They can now be text-based as well as voice-enabled using Python's natural language processing.

It's battle-tested and ready to use.
Python provides us with a massive, battle-tested, and ready-to-use toolkit that can perform all of the hard lifting for us: there are packages for loading and manipulating data, displaying data, translating inputs into a numerical matrix, and actual machine learning and assessment. All you need to do is write the code that will hold everything together. As simple as that.

Business applications

Python has grown increasingly popular for developing commercial applications because of its speed, scalability, and productivity. Python is used by businesses across industries to build online apps, analyze data, and automate operations. Furthermore, enterprise-size firms such as Google, YouTube, and PayPal rely on this coding language for large-scale data operations, among others. Python is an excellent choice for data-driven applications, such as Spotify.

Python's Visualization Approach

Python includes a large number of libraries, some of which are good visualization tools. However, ML Developers must underline that in AI, Deep Learning, and Data Science, the ability to express data understandably is essential. Python has many useful tools for charting data, the most well-known of which is Matplotlib. Seaborn is another excellent piece of software that produces a much more visually appealing plot and also makes use of Matplotlib as its base layer.

1. **Seaborn:**
   Seaborn helps with visualizing statistical correlations. Statistical analysis is used to determine how variables in a dataset are related and how those relationships are influenced by other factors.

2. **Matplotlib:**
   It is a powerful charting toolkit for Python and its extension NumPy. PyPlot is a Matplotlib module that provides a MATLAB interface for Python. Matplotlib enables users to generate publication-quality 2D visualizations from their data.

Python's adaptivity (and ability to merge)
Python supports functional, object-oriented, and imperative programming styles, allowing Machine Learning professionals to focus on the technique that is best for them. Because of its flexibility, it creates a safe environment for developers and reduces the likelihood of errors. When it comes to delivering project or digital product results, the ability to integrate with other languages is critical. Python for Machine Learning is used on the backend to provide the user interface. It can be called out by any other

language to produce a quick and reliable product.

Python, as a general-purpose language, can perform a wide range of complex machine-learning tasks and allows you to quickly create prototypes that allow you to evaluate your solution against machine-learning objectives.

Chapter 5

What Are the Most Challenging Parts of Learning Python for Machine Learning?

The most difficult components of learning Python for machine learning depend on your starting point. Assume you already know how to program with Python. In that instance, using Python for machine learning is simply adding another tool to your existing toolset, utilizing a programming language you already know. If you have no prior experience programming in Python, you should begin by learning the Python programming foundations before learning Python for machine learning.

Python is regarded as a simple programming language, but knowing another language makes the process even easier. The hardest part of learning any programming skill or language is mastering it, which requires practice. Hands-on experience is essential for learning Python for machine learning, but it can be difficult and frustrating if you encounter questions or other obstacles.

How Does Learning Python for Machine Learning Compare to Other Languages?

Python, Java, and R are prominent programming languages for data research. Each coding language has advantages and disadvantages, which this section examines in depth. This section also compares the difficulty of learning each of these programming languages.

Java is a concurrent, general-purpose programming language that is based on classes and object-oriented design. Java is best suited for large-scale projects, although it does not perform as well as Python or R for statistical monitoring. Java is not regarded as complex or difficult to learn.

Python is the most adaptable choice for workflow integrations, allowing you to combine data analysis and statistical methods into a web app or production environment. Python modules like as sci-kit-learn and PyBrain can be used to create prediction engines and models that can be readily integrated into production environments. Python is regarded as a beginner-friendly coding language; but, like with any programming language, hands-on experience is required to commit abilities to memory.

R was created to perform sophisticated statistical analysis. This computer language is good for data science reporting because it can generate high-quality images and charts; nevertheless, R runs slower than Python or Java. R is considered a tough programming language to master.

Whether you want to learn Java, Python, or R, having an instructor take you through real-world, hands-on projects will help you learn more quickly and consolidate your abilities.

Chapter 6

Mastering Python for Machine Learning

Laying the Foundation: Python Basics
Before getting into the complexity of machine learning, be sure you have a firm understanding of Python principles. Codecademy, W3Schools, and Python.org provide good basic courses. Familiarize yourself with syntax, data types, loops, and functions to establish a solid foundation for your trip.

Scikit-Learn is your gateway to machine learning:
Scikit-Learn is a powerful Python machine-learning library. Dive into its documentation and tutorials to learn about important concepts including data preprocessing, model training, and evaluation. Begin by implementing classic methods such as linear regression before progressing to more complex techniques.

Exploring Python Libraries: The Powerhouse Ecosystem.

Python's strength is its robust library ecosystem. Begin with the core ones, such as NumPy and Pandas, which are required for numerical operations and data manipulation. As you continue, explore Matplotlib and Seaborn for data visualization. These libraries provide the foundation for your future machine learning and artificial intelligence projects.

Hands-on Projects: Applying Theoretical Knowledge

Theoretical knowledge is more effective when utilized in real-world situations. Kaggle, for example, provides datasets and competitions, allowing you to put your talents to the test while also learning from the global data science and machine learning communities. Building projects is an important step toward acquiring hands-on experience.

Unleashing Deep Learning with TensorFlow and PyTorch

TensorFlow and PyTorch are useful tools for getting started with neural networks and deep learning. TensorFlow, which is commonly used in production, and PyTorch, known for its dynamic computing graph, provide different approaches to handling challenging ML challenges.

Community Engagement: Participating in the ML and AI Discourse

Active engagement in online communities is essential for ongoing learning. Platforms such as Stack Overflow, Reddit (r/MachineLearning), and GitHub provide forums for asking questions, receiving advice, and sharing information. Networking with professionals from these communities can provide a variety of insights.

Attending Workshops and Webinars to Learn from Experts

Stay informed about workshops and webinars offered by industry experts. Meetups and similar platforms frequently offer events where you can learn from specialists, ask questions, and keep up with the newest industry trends. These activities provide a unique opportunity for interactive learning.

Staying Updated and Experimenting: Accepting Change

Machine learning is a dynamic field that is always evolving. Regularly read blogs, follow researchers on platforms such as arXiv and experiment with novel techniques. Cultivate a curious mindset and don't be afraid to test out new ideas in your initiatives. Accept change as an essential component of the learning process.

In essence, mastering Python for ML is a never-ending process distinguished by curiosity, perseverance, and a desire to keep current on developing developments. As you explore Python's vast terrain, you will discover its revolutionary capability in transforming industries and addressing complicated challenges. Embrace the challenges, enjoy the process, and let Python guide you through the fascinating realm of machine learning and artificial intelligence.

Final Thoughts

Machine learning algorithms drive innovation and efficiency in a variety of industries, including healthcare, banking, transportation, and entertainment. As we've seen, getting started in machine learning necessitates a solid background in mathematics and programming, a thorough understanding of machine learning methods, and hands-on experience working on projects.

Whether you're interested in becoming a data scientist, a machine learning engineer, an AI specialist, or a research scientist, there's a plethora of chances in the field of machine learning. With the correct tools and resources, anyone can study machine learning and contribute to this exciting subject.

Machine learning is more than a buzzword; it's a powerful tool that's transforming the way we live and work. Understanding what machine learning is, how it works, and how to get started is the first step toward a future in which you can use machine learning to solve complicated issues and make a significant difference.

www.ingramcontent.com/pod-product-compliance
Lightning Source LLC
Chambersburg PA
CBHW072056230526
45479CB00010B/1099